D1716415

EXTINCT
FACT FILES

EXTINCT

FACT FILES

SIMON FURMAN

First published in October 2001 by Channel 4
Books, an imprint of Pan Macmillan Ltd,
20 New Wharf Road, London N1 9RR,
Basingstoke and Oxford.

Associated companies throughout the world.

www.panmacmillan.com

ISBN 0 7522 1992 8

9 8 7 6 5 4 3 2 1

A CIP catalogue record for this book is
available from the British Library.

Original illustrations by Steve D. White
Design and typesetting by Jane Coney
Printed by Bath Press

This book accompanies the
television series Extinct, made by
Wall to Wall Television Ltd for
Channel 4.

CONTENTS

INTRODUCTION 8

ICE AGE 10

Mammoth 20

Sabre-toothed Tiger 36

Irish Elk 52

MODERN TIMES 70

Dodo 76

Great Auk 94

Tasmanian Tiger 110

CONCLUSION 126

INTRODUCTION

We share this planet with millions of different creatures – a huge variety of mammals, birds, reptiles, fish and insects. Our world, it seems, can accommodate any number of different species. But the shocking fact is: of all the species ever to have existed on Earth, around 99.9 per cent of these are now dead, gone…

EXTINCT!

Let's face it, evolution is flawed. The way in which living creatures adapt to changes in climate, food supply and geography is just not all it's cracked up to be. It takes thousands, even millions, of years to get an animal kitted out with exactly the right genetic gear it needs to survive, and suddenly — it's history. Take the six creatures re-created by the Extinct team: the mammoth, the sabre-toothed tiger, the Irish elk, the dodo, the great auk and the Tasmanian tiger. They were all superbly adapted for the environment in which they lived, and yet somehow they failed to survive. Why? What went wrong?

Let's turn back the clock...

PART ONE
ICE AGE

'CENE OF THE CRIME

Right now, we live in a period of Earth's history known as the Holocene, which kicked off about 10,000 years ago. This may seem like a long time, but in terms of the geological history of the planet it's less than the blink of an eye. Earth is around 4,500 MILLION years old, and life (very basic life) dates back 3,000 million years. We didn't come on the scene until just a couple of million years ago.

In this first part of the book, we're going to turn the spotlight on a period in Earth's history known as the Pleistocene. This began about 1.8 million years ago and ran all the way up to the start of the Holocene. The Pleistocene was a time of great ecological and geographical upheaval. It's what weather fore-casters today call 'changeable'. The biggest changes of all came in the 'ice ages', when massive ice sheets (glaciers) covered much of the globe for thousands of years at a time.

The Pleistocene saw the introduction of a new kind of mammal perfectly adapted to these harsh conditions. These mammals included the mammoth, the woolly rhinocer-os, the giant ox, the sabre-toothed cat family and the giant deer family. Collectively they were the ice age mammals, or 'megafauna' – so the extinction of these incredible animals is called the megafaunal extinction.

TIMELINE

Hadean (4500 mya*)
Earth is formed.

Archaean (3800 mya)
Water appears.

Mesozoic Era (230 mya)
**Reptiles and dinosaurs rule
the Earth.**

Paleocene (65 mya)
**Dinosaurs die out. Mammals
become dominant.**

*mya = millions of years ago **ya = years ago

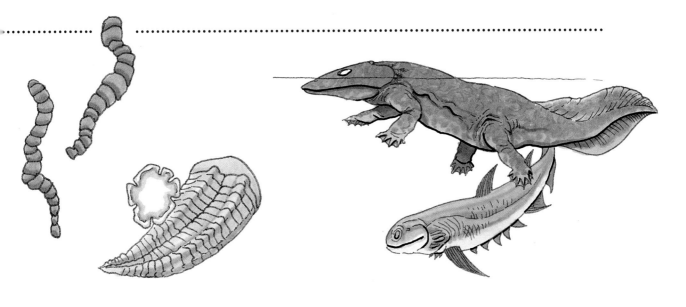

Proterozoic Era (2500 mya)
Basic life evolves.

Paleozoic Era (500 mya)
The first vertebrates,
jawless fishes, appear.

Pleistocene (1.8 mya)
Humans evolve. Periods of global
cooling (ice ages) occur.

Holocene (11,000 ya)**
Modern humans start to
make a mess of the planet.

THE ICE AGES

Ice ages represent periods of time when large areas of the planet were covered with ice sheets, or glaciers. Today, we tend to think of polar ice caps as normal, but there were long periods in Earth's history when the Arctic and Antarctic regions were free from ice. Our planet alternates between periods of global warming and global cooling, during which time the ice sheets advance or retreat.

When glaciers move, they leave plenty of evidence behind, especially after they have melted. As the ice sheet advances, it scours the surface rock, and as it recedes, it leaves behind vast gouges (which often fill with glacial melt-water) in the landscape. Also left behind are piles of debris (known as moraines).

Smaller debris from the glaciers, rich in minerals, flows out with the floodwater from the thawing ice and forms lakes and rivers. As some of these dry out, the dust left behind is blown far and wide. This settles and becomes highly nutritious soil, or loess.

The last main ice age covered large expanses of Canada, North America, northern Europe and the United Kingdom, and parts of Asia. It peaked at around 18,000 years ago, after which the world gradually started to warm up.

By around 10,000 years ago, the last great ice age was almost over. There was another brief cold snap (for just a few hundred years), but overall the forecast was good.

Unless, of course, you were a mega-faunal mammal...

THE MAMMOTH

Fast Facts

Columbian mammoth
(*Mammuthus columbi*)

Big!

Over 4.2 metres tall at shoulder-height, and built like a tank; and weighing over 10 tonnes (the same as 130 adult humans).

Extinct!

For the last 10,000 years or so.

Adaptable!

Equally at home in the frozen north or the warmer south.

Trunk!

Used mainly for feeding, it could move, manipulate and break all kinds of objects. Two finger-like projections at the tip, for delicate operations.

Tusks!

Grown in a distinctive 'twist' shape, they could be up to 5 metres long. Used for display and fighting.

Teeth!

Replaced six times during its life, each set progressively bigger than the last. A single tooth could weigh up to 1.8

HAIR TODAY, GONE TOMORROW

The mammoth is one of the oldest and longest-lived of the giant mammals that dominated the last few million years. It belongs to a family group known as proboscideans, which basically means having a big or extended nose. Mammoths are related to the modern elephant.

Twenty-five thousand years ago, mammoths ranged over millions of square kilometres of the northern hemisphere. The nature of the main land masses was very different from today. Then, there was a gradual migration across continents from southern Europe, through Siberia to North America and Mexico.

The ancestral mammoth, Mammuthus meridionalis, dates from around 1.5 million years ago. Three distinct types of mammoth evolved from the ancestral mammoth:

The mammoth was, quite simply, a prehistoric tank. Strong, bigger than any other creature of the time, resourceful and perfectly at home in any number of ice age environments.

However, the traditional image of the mammoth striding across a bleak, snowbound landscape can be misleading. Mammoths mainly inhabited dry, grassy plains, rich in many

The older European steppe mammoth, Mammuthus trogontherii, was a true giant at over 4.5 metres tall and weighing 12 tonnes.

varieties of grass and vegetation. Temperatures were certainly colder than today, but the mammoth had evolved over many thousands of years to suit these conditions.

For example, in northern Europe and Asia, at the peak of the last ice age, the woolly mammoth's fur consisted of long, coarse outer guard hairs and an undercoat of densely packed bristles. Its skin was 1.25–2.5 centimetres thick, with a thick layer of fat beneath it for extra insulation.

The more familiar (and smaller) woolly mammoth, Mammuthus primigenius, had a distinctive hairy coat.

In contrast, the more southerly Columbian mammoth had fewer layers of insulation. Living in a warmer climate, it did not need to conserve so much heat and so could afford to be bigger.

So, as it migrated, the mammoth evolved. Even if conditions changed drastically, or a new threat was introduced into its environment, it seemed the mammoth could just roll on and adapt.

Between 12,000 and 10,000 years ago, the last major ice age was drawing to a close. Mammoths had survived everything the

The Columbian mammoth was a descendant of the steppe mammoth with less body hair and fat.

planet could throw at them for millions of years. So why, just as the last ice age was ending and the world was warming up, did the mammoth die out?

Did the changes in the planet finally overtake them? Did the end of the ice age mean the end of the mammoth?

Let's look a little closer at the world the mammoth inhabited…

WHERE THE MAMMOTH ROAM

If scientists are correct, and the last mammoths were those furthest south, then it's here we should focus our attention. What was life like in south-western America around 11,000 years ago?

PICTURE THE SCENE…

A vast lake, somewhere in the region of Rapid City, South Dakota. It is late afternoon and birds and animals, including American camels, short-faced bears and wild dogs, have gathered to drink and bathe.

The dry, savanna-like landscape is a mosaic of different coloured grasses. The area is dotted with herbaceous plants, shrubs and small trees such as spruce and water birch. The bulk of these follow the course of a narrow, snaking river, hugging the banks. Vast, sandstone mountains the colour of terracotta rise up to the west.

The shriek and spit of jousting carrion birds, fighting over the remains of a long-dead bison, are suddenly drowned out by what at first appears to be a rumble of thunder. The ground shudders and shakes as the noise builds, startling a flock of wading birds that then take to the air all together, squawking.

The mammoth herd, some twenty strong, thunders into view moments later.

The mammoth's body is distinctive, with its large, domed head, neck hump and sloping back. But it is its sheer size and bulk that take the breath away. At the forefront of the herd is the dominant female. Elephant society is matriarchal, and family groups are always led by one experienced female.

The matriarch inspects the scene. Satisfied that any threat is minimal, and that vulnerable youngsters are well protected by their mothers and aunts, the matriarch bellows the all-clear. The herd, thirsty after their long trek across the prairie, heads down to the water's edge to drink. As they move, enormous clouds of dust are stirred into the air, and smaller animals scatter to avoid being crushed underfoot. The long, curving tusks of the mammoth are imposing enough on their own, but the powerful trunk can also cause injury or death.

Water is essential, but the herd will not stay here long. Food is always a major priority for the mammoth, and the search for fresh forage will continue well into the night.

Mammoths spent more than three-quarters of their lives just looking for food and eating it. That meant up to twenty hours out of every day! To sustain its massive bulk, the mammoth needed over 350 kilograms of forage a day.

Like modern elephants, mammoths were herbivores, eating only vegetation. For the more northern mammoths this meant large amounts of coarse, tundra grasses. For the Columbian mammoth, the diet would have been a little more varied. Grass was supplemented by sagebrush, water birch, blue spruce, juniper and other local flora.

At first, scientists were uncertain exactly what made up the Columbian mammoth's diet. In the frozen north, mammoth remains often came complete with preserved dinners in their stomachs. But further south, only bones remained. Then Bechan Cave in southern Utah provided the missing pieces of the puzzle. Inside, a mammoth 'dung blanket' was discovered, about 40 centimetres thick and with a total volume of over 227 cubic metres. This contained all the fossilized plant evidence scientists needed to pin down the Columbian mammoth's diet.

The mammoth mainly fed using its trunk, which acted like a free hand. Lined with strong muscles, it could move, break and manipulate trees, bushes and long grass. The mammoth's trunk had a further refinement, not found in modern elephants. Two small projections at the tip acted like a finger and thumb, for more delicate plucking operations. Tusks could be used like ploughs, to dig up roots and tubers from the ground.

Grass is a very tough food, and strong teeth were needed to deal with it. The mammoth had four shoe-box sized teeth in its mouth, two upper and two lower. Each of these molar teeth had ridges of sharp enamel, which cut up the food as it was chewed. During the course of its life, the mammoth went through six sets of teeth, each progressively bigger than the last. As a tooth wore out, another was waiting behind it to move into place, almost like a dental conveyor belt.

And yet still the mammoth needed extra help to digest its food. Around 160 litres of water per day washed it down, and mammoths relied on microscopic bacteria and protozoa in their digestive systems. These single-celled organisms broke down the tough cellulose found in grass.

Mammoths were hugely efficient eating machines, and their size meant that even the deadliest of ice age predators gave them a wide berth.

But did a new hunter arrive on the scene, one for whom even the mighty mammoth was fair game?

OVER THE HILL… OR OVERKILL?

Overkill is a term that describes a species hunted to extinction. We can be reasonably sure that the mammoth was hunted by early humans. In Clovis, Arizona, stone spear tips were unearthed, some still lodged in the remains of mammoths.

Clovis humans (named after the site) entered America around 12,000 years ago, and spread rapidly south. Excavations at Clovis sites have revealed that these early settlers used mammoth bones to make tools and even dwellings. Certainly a single mammoth carcass would have provided a vast amount of food, around 2,000 kilograms of meat. But how exactly do you go about hunting such a huge and dangerous creature?

PICTURE THE SCENE…

A plain in southern Arizona. It is dusk. A lone male mammoth moves steadily across the wide, open terrain, feeding as he goes. Sight is not the mammoth's strongest sense, and by now he is mostly feeling his way along, using his trunk to probe and sniff.

Ahead, an area covered by branches and brushwood looms. The mammoth moves

towards it, unaware of the danger it represents. Until, suddenly, the ground collapses under its colossal weight, and the mammoth pitches forward helplessly into the camouflaged pit underneath.

The pit is over 4 metres deep, and the mammoth disappears almost completely into it. He struggles, but the sides are steep and sloped inwards. His legs are pinned. The mammoth bellows in frustration, flailing his trunk.

From nearby cover, a small hunting party emerges. Six Clovis humans armed with spears and heavy rocks gather at the top of the pit. The distinctive spearheads are stone, sharpened to a point and secured to the long shafts with pitch and sinew. The hunters know exactly which vital areas on the great beast to target. They, and their tribe, will eat well tonight.

But did early humans bring something else with them, something other than spears?

GROWING PAINS

Mammoths, like today's elephants, are highly social animals. Adult herds often numbered twelve or more, and these were almost entirely female, consisting of blood relatives – sisters, aunts or nieces. Adult males lived more solitary lives, roaming either singly or in groups of twos and threes. In early summer, though, males and females would come together to mate.

Competition for a female was sometimes fierce, and these otherwise placid animals could easily turn on each other. In such a situation, tusks would be used first for display… and then for attack!

PICTURE THE SCENE…

New Mexico, 10,000 years ago… A female mammoth is being courted by two competing males. Each bellows a challenge at the other. Then, tusks are raised and brandished. The female could now show she prefers one or the other male. (This might discourage the competition and avoid a fight.) The size and condition of a male's tusks are good indicators of his potential as a father.

In this case, though, there is nothing to choose between the two males and neither is prepared to back down. The males start to butt heads and spar with each other. Then tusks are locked together, and a twisting contest ensues. Occasionally, a whole tusk will be broken off during such battles, and the injured male will be forced to retreat. Here, though, neither male can gain the upper hand – or tusk!

The battle becomes increasingly violent, and the males are now using their tusks to gouge and dig. When they thrust them upwards, crash them down from above or swipe them sideways, the tusks can be lethal weapons. Unless one male now relents, the battle will be to the death.

The gestation period for mammoth females was around twenty-two months, so mating in the early summer allowed for calves to be born in the spring of the year after next. A female mammoth would give birth to one solitary calf.

At first, a calf was fed only on its mother's milk. This would be the only time in its life when the mammoth took food directly into its mouth. Some plant food was taken after only a few months, and within two to three years the calf would be fully weaned – ready to feed for itself. By this time, the mother would be ready to breed again.

On reaching maturity at around ten years old, the male calves tended to strike out on their own, while the females would remain with the herd. These all-female family groups would remain closely knit. If a mother died while her calf was still young, the calf would be adopted by a relative.

THE BITTER END

In the end, there are no hard and fast answers, but we can at least look at the evidence and take an educated guess or two.

What we do know is this:

Between 12,000 and 10,000 years ago the world started warming up in a serious way. These changes in climate occurred in a relatively short space of time, and led to a major shift in the patterns of vegetation.

The mammoth needed to eat a lot, and specific types of vegetation it fed on started disappearing. To the north, the nutrient-rich steppe tundra was replaced by a more boggy variety. In the south, the milder, wetter weather encouraged the growth of vast forests of oak, elm and maple. The mammoth was just not built for forest feeding – it needed wide open spaces. Specialist feeders, such as deer, took over. The rich, varied grasslands in which the mammoth roamed scaled down or disappeared, replaced in some cases by desert conditions. The mammoth could no longer cope. The habitat that had supported it for millions of years was almost gone.

However, ice ages had come and gone before, and the mammoth had always survived. It was amazingly adaptable and,

though the herds might have thinned down in size, it's unlikely they'd have vanished completely. We know that the Columbian mammoth moved further south, to Mexico, where there was still abundant food.

Also, if there was an absence of food, mammoth remains from this period would show signs of nutritional stress. The fossil remains from the Mexico area show none of this.

> So what else was going on about this time?

> Well, for one thing, humans had appeared on the scene. Did overkill come into play at this point?

There are two problems with the idea of overkill. For a start, mammoths were huge creatures. No matter how well armed or organized the early American humans were, there were simply easier ways to get a good meal. There's lots of evidence that Clovis humans ate fish and small game such as rabbits. If they hunted, it was for deer and bison. There's comparatively little hard evidence of mammoth hunting. It's far more likely that Clovis hunters simply scavenged from already dead mammoths, especially for their bones.

It's also difficult and self-defeating to hunt an entire species to extinction. Normally, hunter and prey exist in a well-maintained natural balance. After all, if the prey is gone for good, hunters can no longer hunt it. It's also hard to believe humans could have hunted a creature like the mammoth in sufficient numbers to wipe it out.

So if not entirely due to the change in climate, and not just down to over-hunting, what?

The new theory centres on something called a hyperdisease.

In the sixteenth century, Spanish conquistadors entered South America in search of new colonies and treasure. The native Aztecs resisted, but in the end it wasn't the Spanish guns or swords that defeated them. It was measles, and the flu. These diseases were unknown in the Americas, and the local people had no immunity to them. They died in their thousands. Could the same sort of thing have happened to the mammoth? Did the humans who swept down across the continent bring with them a disease deadly to

Mammuthus columbi?

Diseases that can jump from one species to another are rare, but not unknown. AIDS, which may have originated in monkeys, is perhaps the most notorious. The Ebola virus is another, and it has a 90 per cent fatality rate.

Even if the disease didn't come from humans directly, it may have come with the dogs and rats that followed them. Fleas, carried by the dogs tamed by Clovis humans, may have infested mammoth hair. Fleas in turn carry diseases such as bubonic plague.

The mammoth, which had never encountered diseases like this, may have been unable to fight off the effects. Add this to the climate change, the reduction in available food, hunting and the thinning of the herd… and you have a plausible explanation for extinction.

Verdict: the mammoth was just too big to out-race the changing planet and escape the impact of humans on its shrinking environment.

THE SABRE-TOOTHED TIGER

Fast Facts

sabre-toothed tiger
(Smilodon fatalis)

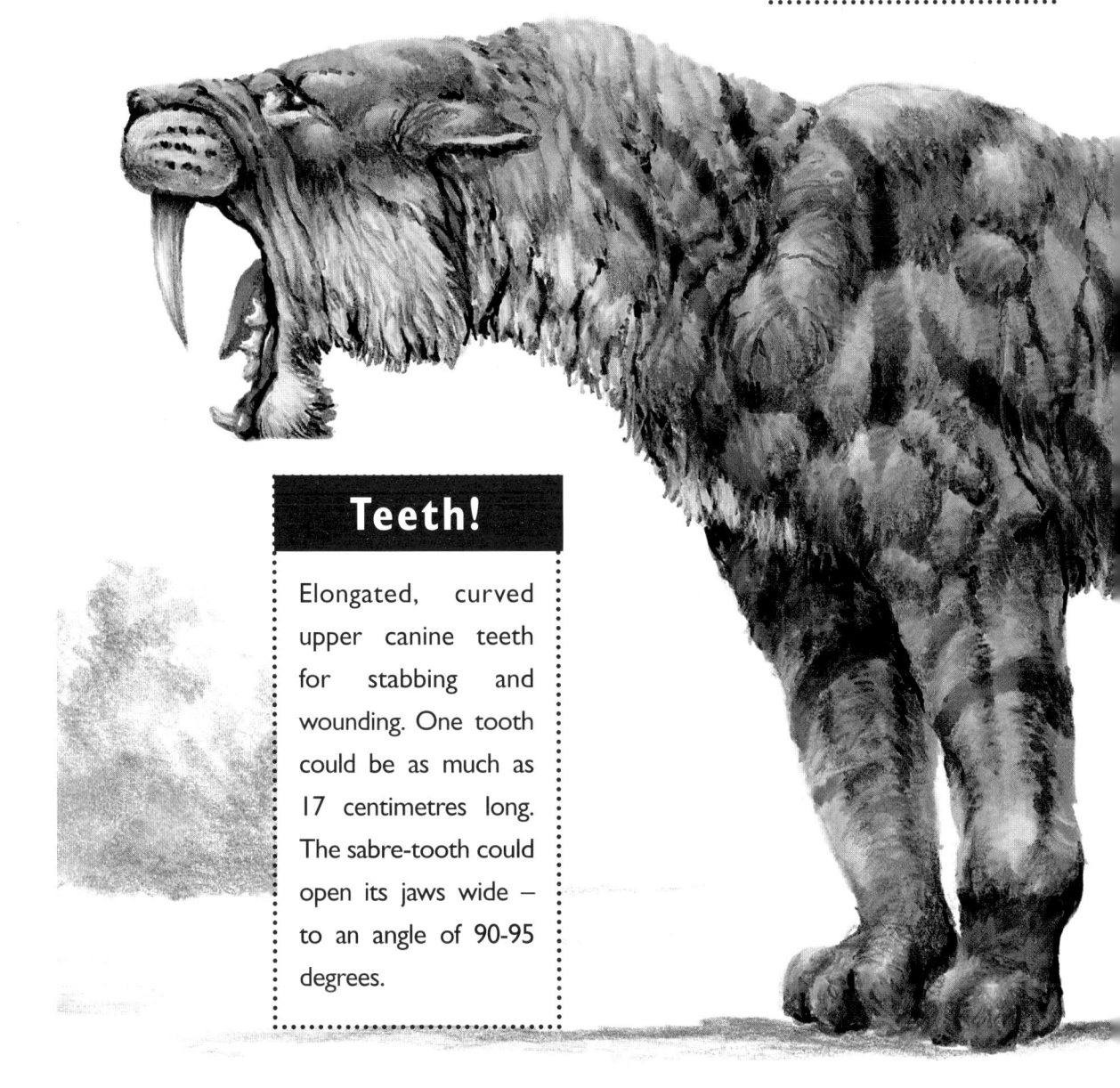

Unchallenged!

It had no direct competition for food, and no real enemies.

Teeth!

Elongated, curved upper canine teeth for stabbing and wounding. One tooth could be as much as 17 centimetres long. The sabre-tooth could open its jaws wide — to an angle of 90-95 degrees.

Deadly!

It was an ambush hunter, and could bring down and kill prey twice its size.

Strong!

Built like a bear, it had immensely muscular forelimbs and neck. It was around 1.5 metres long and weighed around 200 kilograms.

Extinct!

For the last 11,000 years.

Claws!

Razor-sharp, curved and fully retractable, used for spearing its prey and holding it firmly.

TOP CAT

While its canine teeth were named after the distinctively curved sword, the sabre, the sabre-tooth itself actually bore little resemblance to the present-day tiger. Or indeed to any of today's big cats. In fact, sabre-tooths were a part of an entirely different branch of the cat family, known as Machairodonts.

The most immediately striking and best known of the sabre-tooths was Smilodon fatalis, with its huge upper canine teeth and powerful body. Not much bigger than a modern-day lion but twice the weight, Smilodon fatalis was a highly adapted and ruthlessly efficient predator.

The sabre-toothed tiger first appeared over one million years ago.

We can see from reconstructed skeletal remains that sabre-tooths were actually more bear-like than cat-like. They had big, powerful forelegs and thick necks, with a shortened lumbar region in the spinal column. This overall shortening of the body reduced its mobility, but greatly increased its overall strength. Smilodon substituted speed for power.

It is believed that Machairodonts split off from the main cat family (Felidea) around 30 million years ago. Smilodon's direct ancestor was Megantereon, which was about the size of a modern mountain lion and roamed all over the northern hemisphere. About 5 million years ago, Megantereon migrated across a land bridge to the Americas, where it thrived and diversified. Over many generations, this American side of the Machairodont family evolved into Smilodon.

The earliest and smallest of these was Smilodon gracilis, which existed around 2.5 million years ago.

Another ancestor was Smilodon populator, which had the longest canines of all, about 17 centimetres.

Smilodon fatalis first appeared on the scene

Smilodon fatalis was twice as heavy as the modern-day lion.

around one million years ago. It was widespread across North and South America, but never reached Europe or Asia at all.

As sabre-tooths evolved, so their size increased. Normally, there is a direct relationship between the size of a predator and the prey it can hunt. In other words, even the deadliest predators rarely bite off more than they can chew. Unless, of course, you're equipped with deadly sabre teeth!

We know that sabre-tooths hunted early bison, which were much bigger than modern bison (standing at around 1.8 metres and weighing a colossal 1.4 tonnes). As a rule, sabre-tooth's prey was significantly larger than itself, but such hunts came with an element of risk. Despite their size and sharpness, Smilodon's canine teeth were comparatively thin, and could easily be broken off trying to bite a moving, thick-skinned animal. Such an injury would have left Smilodon unable to hunt.

Were Smilodon's incredible canines as much of a liability as they were a bonus?

Let's go on the prowl with the sabre-toothed tiger…

SLOW FOOD

Sabre-tooths were carnivores, or meat-eaters. The American continent of around 12,000 years ago was home to an incredible variety of giant mammals, many of which are now extinct. Mammoths, giant sloths, bison and giant camels all co-existed with Smilodon. Their sheer size made them relatively slow-moving, and so tempting prey for a skilled hunter such as the sabre-tooth.

PICTURE THE SCENE...

The coastal regions of southern California, around 11,000 years ago. Across a wide, grassy plain small herds of bison, giant camels and wild horses graze. Though the herds are not large, they provide a certain amount of safety from the deadly predators that share this lush landscape.

A sudden wind stirs the branches of a nearby cluster of spruce trees, and a grazing camel twitches its head nervously. The woodland settles again, but for long moments the camel's gaze remains fixed on the tree-line, alert for danger. It sniffs the air, but no tell-tale scent is being carried. Once more it lowers its head to the lush, mixed grasses that provide its staple diet.

The camel follows the path of the choicest vegetation towards a nearby water hole. It has now strayed further from the herd than is its usual habit, but the promise of fresh water is enticing.

The sun is high and hot in the cloudless sky.

It passes close to the trees, its earlier caution forgotten. Too late it hears the sudden crack of snapping branches and the tall, surrounding grasses part with a blur of motion. The sabre-tooth's initial pounce becomes a sort of half-gallop as it closes the remaining distance on the startled camel. Though not known for its speed, the sabre-tooth's sheer strength and momentum carry it forward like a runaway truck.

The camel turns to flee, but it is already too late. The sabre-tooth rears up on its hind legs. It wraps its massive forelimbs around the camel's head and neck, sinking its claws in deep. The sabre-tooth uses its considerable weight and power to wrestle the camel to the ground.

Pinned, the camel thrashes, kicking out with a hind leg. But the sabre-tooth has positioned itself carefully, and prepares to deliver the fatal strike. In the process of twisting and bringing the camel to the ground, the sabre-tooth has exposed its prey's neck. It opens its massive jaws and bites down hard. Death is almost instantaneous.

The sabre-tooth then drags the carcass back into the cover of the trees, where it can feed unchallenged by scavengers or other sabre-tooths. It uses its canine teeth to slice the flesh, serrated edges sawing through the animal's tough hide.

An adult sabre-tooth needed around 30 kilograms of meat a week to feed itself, more if it had a family to support. However, the large size of the mammals it hunted meant that relatively few kills were necessary to stave off hunger for days at a time.

This was beneficial for two reasons. First, it took a great amount of energy to wrestle a huge animal like a camel or a bison to the ground. Second, the chances of being injured while hunting were very high. Many of the sabre-tooth bones that have been unearthed show signs of multiple fractures. Even in its death-throes, a bison could

deliver a devastating kick. Some bones were a mangled mess, and yet somehow these sabre-tooths had survived their injuries.

Scientists today are split on whether the sabre-toothed tiger hunted exclusively alone, or occasionally with other sabre-tooths. On the one hand, a solo approach makes sense for an ambush hunter – and the meat would not have to be shared three or four ways. But another theory is that two or three sabre-tooths tackling a bison would have been much more effective. It couldn't have been easy for one sabre-tooth to drag a carcass to cover or to feed uninterrupted in the open. If there were two or three sabre-tooths, one could stand guard while the others fed.

Then there were the terrible injuries that sabre-tooths suffered… and survived. With a broken leg, it would be impossible for it to hunt successfully. But if sabre-tooths hunted in packs, and shared their kills, it would explain why these injured animals survived. Of course, modern cats heal from injuries with incredible speed, and it's likely that sabre-tooths were similarly resilient. So they may simply have healed fast enough to avoid starvation. But the argument goes on, with no firm answers.

Whatever the case, life was good for sabre-tooths 12,000 years ago. Apart from a few scavengers such as vultures, hyenas and dire wolves, the sabre-tooth had little or no competition for food.

But did that situation change?

Did an even more cunning and resourceful hunter challenge the sabre-tooth's position at the top of the food chain?

GROWING PAINS

Very little is actually known about the sabre-tooth's cycle of birth, life and death. With no living or easily identifiable descendants, it's hard to compare behaviour and draw accurate conclusions.

It is likely, though, that sabre-tooths formed small family groups. These family units, a mother and two or more cubs, would have stayed together for at least two years. Sabre-tooth cubs did not develop their actual sabre teeth until well into their second year of life, and so would have been unable to hunt effectively for themselves.

However, the cubs would soon have been big and strong enough to have assisted their mother in bringing down her prey. In the process, they would learn to do so for themselves. As there was no great size difference between male and female sabre-tooths, the mother would certainly have been capable of hunting and supporting her family alone. It's also likely that other female family members, such as nieces or sisters, lived and hunted together.

In many of today's big cat families, the adult male maintains a solo existence, marking out a clearly defined territory as his own. Strategically placed scent-markings warn off competing males. Normally, a male territory such as this would intersect with those of one or more females. The females would defend their territory, the male would defend the females.

That's not to say this is how it worked with sabre-tooths, but it is possible. The bones from sabre-tooth males show evidence of a lot of fighting, much of which was probably

with other male sabre-tooths. However, big prides, like those of modern-day lions, seem unlikely for the sabre-tooth, male or female.

Sabre-tooth males would have used urine or scent-glands in their paws to mark out their territories. This could also be used to exchange information, or identify good hunting grounds.

It's fair to conclude that there was a certain level of sociability, especially with lots of food readily available. But as that changed, how did Smilodon react?

Was it so easy for the sabre-tooth to get food that it grew lazy?

Had it become too specialized?

THE BITTER END

It's rare that we can say with absolute certainty how and why a certain species died out, but with sabre-tooths it's even more inconclusive. However, by looking at what was going on around the animal at the time it disappeared, we can at least point the finger in certain directions.

Between 12,000 and 10,000 years ago the last main ice age was ending, and the world was warming up. There was a major shift in the patterns of vegetation, and in a relatively short space of time much of it had changed or disappeared completely.

In itself, this wouldn't have affected the sabre-toothed tiger at all. After all, it was a carnivore. But it did affect the giant mammals on which it fed. In a big way.

The clues to this huge shift in the planet's eco-system come from a surprisingly small source. The packrat, a tiny rodent, collected little piles of vegetation to make its nest, and glued them together with its urine. These piles of vegetation have been found still preserved in caves today. Scientists could examine them and date the vegetation. It then became clear just how drastically the available plant-life changed over a relatively short time.

As temperatures increased, huge areas dried out. The lush, mixed grasses, shrubs and trees that formed the staple diet of bison, prehistoric horses and camels disappeared. These were replaced by scrub and open, coarse grasslands, which were low in nutrients, or often by deserts. Many rivers and watering holes dried up.

Camels, horses and other giant mammals, the sabre-tooth's chosen prey, started dying out in large numbers. There was simply no longer enough variety of plant-life to support them. And even the plants they did find may well have been slowly poisoning them. Plants produce certain chemicals such as nicotine and capsicum that will poison a herbivore if it eats enough of them. Less variety meant that more of these chemicals were being taken in. Within only a thousand years many species were extinct.

But not all the giant herbivores died out.

We know, for instance, that bison survived, and even thrived. With their four-chambered stomachs, they could digest more low-nutrient

attentions to other, smaller mammals – like the pronghorn, a north American antelope. But these were faster still, and could easily escape… especially when Smilodon could no longer easily lie in wait, hidden.

But was this enough to account for the extinction of an entire species, especially one as resourceful and deadly as the sabre-tooth? Ice ages had come and gone many times before, and yet Machairodonts and their descendants had survived. So why now? What other factor came to bear on the already stressed sabre-tooth population?

Clovis humans were also now hunting bison and the other remaining large mammals, and they were better at it than Smilodon. Whole areas may have been depopulated simply due to over-hunting by man. Sabre-tooths themselves may even have been hunted as food became scarcer.

The combination of less available food and greater competition may have been enough to drive the sabre-tooths to starvation and ultimately extinction. The evidence is largely circumstantial, but the timing of so many large-scale extinctions with man's arrival in the area cannot be ignored.

Verdict: The sabre-toothed tiger was over-specialized in its hunting patterns, unable to react to the sudden changes in climate and the loss of its main sources of food. It ran out of prey.

food. Tiny microbes in their gut allowed them to break down tough grasses. Horses and camels, which both died out, had only one-chambered stomachs.

So why didn't Smilodon just make bison its staple diet? The fact is, bison were also going through some major changes around this time. They got smaller for a start, and quicker. They also started gathering in bigger herds. This was all bad news for Smilodon. Its prey could run faster and escape more easily, and the bigger herds meant there were more watchful eyes.

And with the changing landscape went the trees and shrubs that provided cover for the sabre-tooth. For an ambush hunter, relying on dense foliage and tall grass, this was a disaster.

No doubt Smilodon tried switching its

THE MISSING LINK

Around this time, 12,000 or so years ago, we know that early humans appeared throughout North America. They were highly efficient hunters, equipped with stone-headed throwing spears. And while they may not have directly hunted sabre-tooths, they did hunt its prey.

These Clovis humans (named after the archaeological dig in Clovis, Arizona, which first identified them) spread rapidly across the continent. They were social and well-organized. They knew how to lay traps and how to track and kill the giant mammals on which sabre-tooth fed. They may even have hunted mammoths, something that sabre-tooths rarely did.

For the sabre-tooth, the world had started to change.

PICTURE THE SCENE…

A sabre-tooth female moves belly low through the tall grasses bordering a steep gully. For the past hour, she has been edging closer to a small herd of grazing bison. She is downwind of the herd, and no stray scent has warned them of her approach. For a creature of her size, she moves with elaborate stealth, careful to avoid dry twigs.

Her sandy fur, mottled with darker stripes, provides excellent camouflage. She is all but invisible among the late afternoon's long shadows. Now she is within reach of the nearest bison. It is so close that a single leap will see it in her clutches. She tenses, settling back on her hind legs, bunching her thigh muscles. Her jaw gapes wide…

With no warning her prey bolts, startled. Then she hears it, the sound of raised guttural voices and sticks beating the grass. As the bison turn to run, spears whistle through the air. One animal falls, then another. The remainder are forced down into the gully, and in their panic they tumble and twist down the sharp incline.

The men appear then, and the sabre-tooth roars her anger and frustration, moving to claim one of the fallen bison. But the men stand their ground, jabbing at her with their spears. A hurled stone hits her, cracking a bone. Hurt, limping, she is forced to retreat. She and her cubs will go hungry today.

MORTAL REMAINS

Because of the lack of direct descendants of the sabre-toothed tiger, scientists have had to rely more than ever on fossilized skeletal remains in order to piece together a picture of it.

By reconstructing skeletons and working out how the sabre-tooth's musculature functioned, many pieces of the puzzle have now fallen into place.

Earlier theories about the way in which Smilodon used its huge upper canines have now been rejected. For instance, people once believed that the sabre-toothed tiger survived by drinking the blood of its prey, like a vampire bat. Another theory was that the teeth were for display during the mating season, and not for cutting at all.

The richest fossil evidence of Smilodon has been uncovered at the La Brea tar pits, slap bang in the middle of what is now modern-day Los Angeles.

Tar pits form when crude oil seeps to the surface through cracks in the Earth's crust. It's likely that 11,000 or so years ago the thick, sticky tar was disguised by surface water. Animals coming to drink would have found themselves stuck fast and slowly sinking.

Tar is a natural preservative, and even the smallest, most fragile sabre-tooth bones (from the ear, even the throat) have been found. The bones are in perfect condition, due to the tar and the speed with which they were covered. They didn't rot and they weren't pulled apart by scavengers.

To date, scientists have recovered over a million bones from La Brea, from fifty-nine species of mammal and thirty-five species of birds. It's estimated that the remains of over 2,000 sabre-tooths have so far been uncovered.

Perhaps more answers to the mystery of the sabre-tooth still lie buried there, waiting to be discovered.

THE IRISH ELK

Fast Facts

Irish elk
(Megaloceros giganteus)

Widespread

Earliest specimens date back over 40,000 years, and ranged as far and wide as Europe, Asia and the Middle East.

Antlers!

Spanning up to 4 metres from tip to tip. Used both for display and combat.

Fast!

The Irish elk could run at around 80 kph, and keep up this punishing pace for over fifteen minutes.

Giant!

One of the largest deer species ever. Stood 2 metres tall at shoulder height, was around 2.2 metres long and weighed around 700 kilograms.

Resilient!

Adapted bone and antler structure for maximum durability and strength. Reserve calcium stored in hollow jaw.

Extinct!

For the last 9,000 years or so.

SIZE MATTERS

First, let's shatter one popular myth. The Irish elk
was not Irish, at least not exclusively.

Early ancestors of Megaloceros roamed as far afield as Japan, China, the Middle East and North America, and the Irish elk itself was widespread throughout Europe, northern Asia and North Africa. The name 'Irish' was coined, and stuck, because a large number of excellent, well-preserved fossils were found in lake sediments and peat bogs in Ireland.

The Irish elk's ancestors go back around 400,000 years, but it's really just two periods of time that we need to focus on: From radiocarbon-dating of the fossil bones of the Irish elk, we know that Megaloceros was in Ireland before and after the last major ice age. But never when the region was completely covered by glaciers.

Maybe. But other species survived and thrived (and, yes, evolved) through the ice ages, and Megaloceros was not without a biological trick or two itself. So what else do we know about this incredible creature?

We can tell at a glance that the Irish elk was **BIG**.

In evolutionary terms, big is often a response to the amount of competition. The larger you are, the harder it is for someone to muscle in on your personal feeding ground. But it's also how living creatures demonstrate that they are able to produce strong offspring. The health and well-being of the young means the species is likely to survive over a long period of time.

Then there were the Irish elk's antlers. They were huge, over 4 metres from tip to tip! But could they have been too big?

Not according to size comparisons with modern deer. Despite its name, the Irish elk was not an elk – its closest living relative is the fallow deer. In fact, for a creature of its size the Irish elk's antlers were perfectly in

proportion, and they were undoubtedly very important. To grow them would have taken huge amounts of precious minerals and nourishment, and this was not a one-off deal – the Irish elk shed its antlers and grew a new pair every year.

Were big antlers so important that the Irish elk would risk starvation to grow them?

Before we make too many rash guesses, let's look a little closer at the world the Irish elk inhabited…

Was the ice age itself the cause of the Irish elk's extinction?

WHERE THE ELK ROAM

One thing's for sure – the Irish elk needed to eat. A lot. But what exactly did it feed on, and where do you find a decent 'all you can eat' in the late Pleistocene?

PICTURE THE SCENE...

It's around 10,000 years ago, and you've happened upon a wide open plain (somewhere near modern-day Belfast), covered with rich, dry grassland. Spring is almost here, and the temperature is slowly rising again after a long, cold winter. The 'green-up', or growing season, is about to begin, and around you plant life is starting to bud. There's very little in the way of rain, but the local grass and flora (plant life) have adapted to these arid conditions.

The tough, coarse tundra grass of the ice age has retreated with the glaciers, leaving behind melt-off channels, deltas and loess plains. Willow bushes grow in dense clusters around the edge of the vast expanse of grassland, providing cover and essential nutrients.

From the sheltered valley bottom below, where some fresh, running water has resisted the winter freeze, there is movement and sound. A pack of perhaps twenty Irish elk stags are making their way towards higher ground. With little available food and already malnour-ished after the previous season's mating season, the males are slow and unsteady, desperate now to begin feeding. They must rebuild their reserves of strength, gathering the precious nutrients and chemicals they need to survive.

The old antlers have been shed. The valley floor below is littered with vast, calcified remains. As the new antlers grow, they are protected by 'velvet', which has now begun to fall off in matted clumps.

The all-male pack formation is not a surprise. Stags and does (females) move in their own distinct territories, coming together only perhaps once or twice a year. The does will have spent the winter on higher ground, preferring security over comfort.

Slowly, feeding as they go, the herd moves up to where the does are already gathering. The Irish elk doe is immediately identifiable by her lack of antlers and smaller size. She is perhaps two-thirds as big as a stag. Many does are carrying calves, which will be born in late May, shortly before the full 'green-up'. This is the ideal time to get good milk going, necessary to feed their young.

The next mating season is still some months away, and until that time the priority for the gathering stags is to fatten up, while their new antlers are growing stronger.

Scientists are pretty sure that Megaloceros was a bulk roughage feeder, which really means it ate a lot of grass. How do they know this? Well, there are two main clues.

First, by examining the fossil teeth from several Irish elk skulls, scientists could identify patterns of scratches and wear. These were consistent with a creature that eats large quantities of grass (modern cattle have the same marks). Grass contains microscopic amounts of silica, a sharp, abrasive mineral, which scratches tooth enamel as it is chewed.

Secondly, the shape of the Irish elk's snout is another indicator. Modern deer have quite pointed snouts, because they select and pick food. In comparison, Megaloceros had the broadest, flattest snout of any living or extinct deer. This was useful for 'hoovering' up large quantities of grass when grazing, getting the maximum amount of food intake per bite.

And the Irish elk could eat – big time.

By using size comparisons with modern deer, scientists worked out that the Irish elk needed a colossal 44 kilograms of fresh forage a day to maintain its body weight. Unfortunately, grass was only part of the story.

Shedding, re-growing and maintaining those huge antlers every year was a major drain on the Irish elk's energy reserves. Specific minerals, particularly calcium and phosphorus, were essential to make the antlers strong and healthy. It's likely that Megaloceros consumed a large amount of willow. This bushy shrub has plenty of both chemicals and grew close to the grassland on which the Irish elk grazed.

There's every chance that willow became scarce over time, due to the sheer size of the herd and the amount that was consumed per day.

Did the Irish elk, in its hunger, eventually eat itself out of house and home?

FAST FOOD

The Irish elk was a pack feeder and never strayed far from the main herd. There was a certain amount of strength in numbers. But still, the nature of the Irish elk's feeding pattern meant that it was often exposed, caught out in the open, away from cover. While they dined, the Irish elk were also on the menu...

PICTURE THE SCENE...

A herd of Irish elk stand grazing on a high plain, heads lowered. One, though, stands alert, head raised high to sniff the air. Its large, wide eyes scan for intruders, twitching to and fro, covering as much ground as possible. There is something – a slight movement, a scent – and its nostrils flare, alarmed. It barks a short, sharp warning that galvanizes the herd. A marauding pack of wolves, bellies low in the tall grass, has been spotted.

The advance warning is critical. The Irish elk is a big animal, and while it can run at up to 80 kph, its size means it will take time to reach that speed. If cornered, the Irish elk will use its antlers to gore and its strong forelegs to kick, but its first instinct is to run.

Their heads held low, to minimize wind resistance, the pack takes flight. Twenty or more sets of strong, (relatively) short legs thunder across the plain, rising in low,

contained strides to maximize each pace and minimize costly body lift. The Irish elk's small hooves – adapted for running on hard surfaces – pound the dry ground. Each animal has a strong heart and powerful lungs. They will not be easily caught.

Unable to match the pace set by the herd, the wolves break off their pursuit and go in search of easier prey.

But was there another predator, one the Irish elk could not outrun?

Was Megaloceros hunted... and killed off?

GROWING PAINS

PICTURE THE SCENE...

The mating season has begun, and a mature stag has marked his territory. But suddenly there is a roar. A younger, slightly less mature male is threatening to intrude. The two approach each other cautiously. They start to walk in parallel along one edge of the territory, each stag sizing the other up. Challenges are roared and echoed, antlers are held high for inspection.

If the two are not evenly matched, then the weaker stag will back off. Otherwise, he will be risking serious injury or even death.

In this case, the challenge is accepted and a fight begins. Antlers are dipped and locked, and they start twisting and pushing. Each stag tries to force the other off-balance. The neck, flank and belly are gored. The eyes are protected by large, protruding brow tines on the antlers.

The fight may last five days or more and when it is done the chances are one stag will lie dead. On average, a stag may receive between fifty and sixty wounds per season.

JULY–SEPTEMBER:
THE MATING SEASON.

Stags return to the same traditional rutting grounds year in and year out. There, they stake out territories.

Then a ritual display begins. The stag will strut behind the doe, flipping and dipping his antlers in a precise,

OCTOBER–APRIL: THE LONG WINTER MONTHS.

Exhausted, having eaten little or nothing for the duration of the mating season, the stags move off into more sheltered valleys. Winter starvation is not uncommon, especially among the young and old. The life expectancy of a stag is around thirteen years, of a doe perhaps sixteen years.

MAY–JUNE: CALVES ARE BORN.

Irish elk calves need to be able to match their parents in terms of speed and stamina within only three to four weeks. They need to be physically fit if they are to evade predators and keep up with the herd in its search for food.

At first, a new-born calf is hidden. Its mother returns to feed it only every few days, so as not to draw undue attention to it.

The gestation period for Irish elk females is long, almost nine months, which means the calves are already large at birth. Mother's milk, rich in nutrients, will help it to develop quickly.

almost choreographed dance, bellowing with each swing. He's saying: 'Look, I have good genes – I can grow these huge antlers.'

The peak breeding age for the Irish elk is between four and nine years of age. Usually, only the most physically mature stags lay claim to a territory, but sometimes there is a challenge.

Did the winter die-offs among Irish elk stags start to out number new births?

THE BITTER END

In the end, there are no hard and fast answers.

We cannot say for sure what drove the Irish elk to extinction. Even the experts can't always agree. But if we can't actually rewind the CCTV tape of the late Pleistocene, we can at least look at the evidence we do have and take an educated guess or two.

And sometimes even then the answer isn't clear cut. Sometimes there's a twist in the evolutionary tale.

What we do know is this:

Ten thousand years ago, there was an intense cold snap called the Younger Dryas. Winter temperatures plunged by around 7 or 8 degrees Centigrade. Scientists can tell from plant pollen, found buried with the most recent Irish elk fossils, that the landscape changed dramatically during this period. The dwarf willow bushes, so vital to antler growth, disappeared, and the rich grasslands gave way to sparse tundra and alpine scrub.

The Irish elk's food supply went from ample to scarce in a very short time. What little there was, was spread over huge distances, and even then couldn't always provide enough in the way of nutrients and chemicals.

Depleted and malnourished after mating and fighting, huge numbers of Irish elk were starving to death. What food the herds could find was being eaten at such a rate that whole areas were stripped of vegetation in days. The herd was continually forced to move, covering vast distances in the search for new grazing territories. Many never made it.

The Irish elk did not downsize. We know this because the most recent antlers found are the same size as much older fossils. The need to attract a mate was so important that Irish elk stags continued to use up huge amounts of precious resources in growing large antlers. Osteoporosis, a brittle bone condition caused by lack of calcium, may also have set in.

In short, the Irish elk defied evolution. It did not – or could not – adapt to the changes in its environment.

The cold snap continued, and gradually Megaloceros died out.

Or so scientists thought.

Until, that is, a complete Irish elk skeleton – excavated on the Isle of Man back in 1819 – was given a second look. Scientists discovered that the bones came from a period over a

thousand years after the species had supposedly died out.

And there was another surprise to come. Size comparisons with older specimens revealed that the Isle of Man find was smaller. Here, it seems, evolution had taken its natural course. The Irish elk had downsized.

So if not the cold, if not the lack of food, what, finally, killed off the Irish elk? Sad to say, but it was probably us. Human beings.

We know from fossil evidence (or the lack of it) that Mesolithic (Middle Stone Age) humans never made it to Ireland while the Irish elk was living there. But unlike Ireland, the Isle of Man was at the time still connected to mainland Britain. Scientists believe the Irish elk may well have migrated to northern England and Scotland in search of food, where it was plentiful. It was here that Megaloceros and humans finally crossed paths.

One of the other things we know about Mesolithic humans is that they prized trophies. They used the skulls and antlers of red deer in ceremonies. They may well have actively sought out the more spectacular antlers of the Irish elk for that purpose, too.

It's possible the last Irish elk were simply hunted to extinction.

Whichever way you look at it, it all comes back to the antlers. Perfectly designed to demonstrate good breeding stock and attract a mate, but ultimately a huge liability.

Verdict: one way or another, the Irish elk was wiped out by its own antlers.

MORTAL REMAINS

Much of what we know about the Irish elk is from its fossil remains.

From studying the shape of the Irish elk's jaw, we can say reasonably certainly that it was a plant-eater. By measuring the thickness of a thigh bone and comparing it to modern deer, we can estimate its weight. Soil and pollen collected from around a find can be analysed to identify the local flora. Conclusions can be drawn, but often it is not an exact science.

For a start, while we have many skulls from stags, there are very few female skeletons, fewer still complete. The male's skull is highly distinctive, while the female's can easily be confused with another animal's. Many have probably been found and discarded over the years.

Also, a large number of early reconstructions were made up from more than one Irish elk. And sometimes, where bones were missing, plaster was used to fill the gap. Even horse or cow bones have been known to find their way into Irish elk skeletons.

The cave paintings found in France are another valuable source of information. They show clearly the differences in size and general shape between males and females, and that both sexes had pronounced shoulder humps.

Modern comparisons give us some clue to behaviour and colouring. The North American elk (or wapiti) is lightly coloured, to reflect the summer heat, and the Irish elk

shows other similarities to this breed.

Ireland remains the richest source of Irish elk remains. Over 100 skulls were found at Ballybetagh Bog near Glencullen, about 15 kilometres south of Dublin.

PART TWO
MODERN TIMES

A WHOLE NEW WORLD

As the Pleistocene became the Holocene, so the impact of humans on the planet increased rapidly. Though this current era is only 10,000 years old, it has seen huge advances in human evolution and growth – from early nomadic settlers who relied on stone tools and mud huts, to thriving communities rich in technology, science, culture and sophistication. Humans have dominated the Holocene, even reaching out beyond the planet itself into outer space.

With humankind's new-found thirst for knowledge and experience came a greater curiosity about the planet itself. In particular, the nature of evolution and, ultimately, the concept of extinction.

Scientist Charles Darwin (1809–82) paved the way with his landmark work, The Origin of Species. His theory that all life on Earth evolved from earlier, often very different, species directly opposed the Church-held views on divine creation. In the decades that followed, scientists such as Gregor Mendel, James Dewey Watson and Francis Crick provided an understanding of chromosomes, genes and DNA, the building blocks of evolution.

Meanwhile, humankind spread rapidly across the planet. Advances in communication and transportation meant that previously inaccessible parts of the world could be reached, new frontiers and trade routes established.

But however well-intentioned humankind's expansion and colonization of the globe might have been, it wasn't always beneficial. In many cases, exploration became exploitation.

THE DODO

Fast Facts

dodo
(*Raphus cucullatus*)

Extinct!

For over 300 years.

Flightless!

With no predators, and food generally available, the dodo no longer needed its wings.

Sturdy!

Reserves of fat, stored in the rump, meant the dodo could survive the long months when dangerous cyclones lashed its island home.

Beak!

Tough, long and hooked at the tip. Perfect for digging out tough seeds – or seeing off unwanted intruders.

Big!

Larger than a full-grown turkey. The dodo weighed up to 20 kilograms and stood 80 centimetres high. And yet it evolved from a tiny pigeon.

Nimble!

The dodo's powerful legs meant it could move fast, dodging through dense forested terrain.

SUPER-PIGEON

The popular view of the dodo is that it was fat, slow and stupid. In fact, the dodo is famous for only one thing – being dead. The phrase 'dead as a dodo' has long been applied the world over to just about anything's that's died.

No one is absolutely certain when the dodo first appeared – it was anywhere from 100,000 to 3 million years ago. The dodo was unique to just one area of the world, the small island of Mauritius in the Indian Ocean.

Recent DNA testing (on a preserved dodo beak) has charted the bird's evolutionary course all the way back to an unlikely ancestor. Its closest relative is likely to be a pigeon native to Indonesia (nearly 5,000 kilometres east of Mauritius). Modern pigeons migrate by island-hopping, and it is believed that the dodo's ancestors flew in stages to Mauritius along a now submerged chain of islands.

Better equipped to cope with lean times.

But what happened when it got there? What made it get a whole lot bigger and stop using its wings?

What the migrant pigeon discovered on Mauritius was nothing short of paradise,

Less competition for food or territory.

pigeon paradise. There were absolutely no predators and lots of food. And what's more, the food was all at ground level. Suddenly, it just didn't really need its wings.

In birds that can fly, the muscles vital to wing power amount to around 32 per cent of total body weight. If they're not used, it's a huge waste of precious energy. Over many generations, the pigeon's wings withered or simply didn't grow with the rest of its body.

Its skeleton also went through a number of changes. Its keel (the bone structure to which the major flight muscles are attached) shortened. Its neck became longer, and the breast (the tasty bit on a chicken) toughened and reduced in size. Its femur (leg bone) tilted downwards, making it stand more upright. Its feathers became less streamlined, more fluffy.

It became the dodo.

**But was the dodo
too specialized?**

**Was this a case of evolutionary
short-sightedness?**

Without functional wings, the dodo's body no longer needed to be lightened for flight. It could now afford to be big and reap the benefits that size brings:

Slower, more efficient rate of energy consumption, which meant it could survive extremes of temperature and climate.

DODO ISLAND

The blundering image of the dodo comes mostly from early accounts written by the Dutch sailors who first encountered it. They called it Dodaarsen (fat bottom!).

In the late 1500s, the Dutch were opening up new trade routes to the Far East. The perilous journey took them past the dreaded Cape of Good Hope, at the tip of South Africa. Treacherous storms battered their ships, and in 1598 five of them were blown far off course. The lush, tropical island they sighted promised rest, shelter... and food.

PICTURE THE SCENE...

The island of Mauritius, 400 years ago. It is early in the year, summer in this part of the world. The rainforests that spread down from distant, towering mountain peaks to the sandy beaches below are full of fruit and vegetation. It is hot in this tropical jungle during the day, too hot to move.

The ebony trees that form the bulk of the forest are tall and slender. There's a lot of room between them to forage among the rich undergrowth. The forest floor is awash with grass and leaves. Exotic trees such as Latania or Pandanus have ripe fruits growing on their trunks, conveniently and enticingly near to the ground.

As evening draws nearer, the temperature begins to drop, and from the shade of the nearby palm trees a male dodo emerges. The cool sea breezes have kept the worst of the

and jab at unwelcome fellow feeders.

Strange sounds draw the dodo's attention. On the beach, a party of men, Dutch sailors blown off-course, are chopping wood, throwing the kindling on to a crackling fire. They are very thin and pale. Their journey has been long and arduous, and their food rations ran out over a week ago. One sailor ventures further into the trees, in search of fruit or edible tubers. Wary, unsure of what wild animals lurk in the dense undergrowth, he carries his musket at the ready.

Curious, perhaps even a little put out that his territory is being disturbed in this way, the dodo moves closer.

Too close.

By 1638, forty years after this encounter, the Dutch had established a small colony on Mauritius. It was a staging post they called Fort Hendrik. Its primary purpose was to provide rest and relief for sailors bound for the Far East. But Fort Hendrik was also used to farm, harvest and ship out the famous Mauritius ebony. Back in the Netherlands, the ebony was used to make fine furniture and piano keys.

day's heat at bay, and now he is ready to feed.

The dodo stands tall, upright. His plumage is a dull, bluish grey and half-developed. In some places, especially the head and neck, feathers are absent altogether. A few upright, jutting feathers on the rump are fluffed up, as if for display. Despite his size, the dodo can move with surprising speed and agility – his legs are strong and well developed. His beak is long and ridged, with a sharp hook at its tip. He will use it to snap

Did the Dutch colonists destroy the dodo's environment... and the dodo with it?

FAT OF THE LAND

The dodo was a highly efficient feeder, adapted to take full advantage of the wide range of foodstuffs available. Fruit, seeds, buds, grass, leaves... it ate almost anything and everything. Little wonder it got big.

And the dodo didn't limit itself to the local flora. Mauritius is a volcanic island, with highly acidic soil, so there was little or no calcium in the dodo's daily diet (essential in order to produce strong eggshells). In order to get its daily calcium intake, the dodo would use its powerful beak to snap up and consume large quantities of crabs, coral and snails.

To further aid digestion, the dodo would swallow small pebbles in order to grind the food in its stomach. These 'gizzard stones', as they are known, were especially useful when it came to dealing with shells.

We know the dodo was a big eater, but was it actually fat? Much of what we know about the dodo's physical shape is based on the work of early Dutch painters. But often these images were caricatures, based on second- or third-hand information or accounts. The very first artists to sketch the dodo depicted a much slimmer creature.

In order to prepare for lean times, the dodo would spend the summer putting on extra fat, which it stored in its rump. It could then draw on this storehouse of essential nutrients when food was scarce. So it would have varied quite a bit in size from one season to the next. But experts who have tested the strength of fossil leg bones think its average weight was probably around 15–20 kilograms.

All the evidence seems to suggest the dodo wasn't slow, stupid or fat. But we know the dodo was still hunted, captured and killed by the Dutch settlers.

So was the dodo hunted to extinction?

FOOD FOR THOUGHT

To starving Dutch seamen, a big bird like the dodo must have promised a feast. But was the dodo actually fingerlickin' good?

PICTURE THE SCENE...

A beach on Mauritius, 1598. A group of painfully thin Dutch sailors sit around a camp fire, over which a dodo carcass roasts. The fire spits and crackles as it is splashed with sizzling fat, and a pungent, oily and unpleasant aroma fills the air. The sailors are having a hard time finding meat on the dodo they can stomach.

The breast, normally the most tender and tasty part of a fowl, is tough and barely edible. Most of the meat is on the rump, and even that is mostly fat. The flavour is cloying and over rich, and not at all palatable. To get any kind of meal at all, the sailors are forced to eat it barely cooked.

Eventually the bird is discarded, less than half eaten. At first light the search will begin for something more familiar and less sickening on which to dine.

Excavations at Fort Hendrik have revealed the bones of turtles, sea cows and small birds, but no dodo bones. Whatever the early Dutch settlers were eating, it wasn't the dodo. At least, not by choice.

GROWING PAINS

PICTURE THE SCENE...

The female dodo first inspects the nest-building materials. They must meet her exacting standards.

The male has already begun a ritual dance. His feathers are puffed up, his head is bobbing up and down, and he is flapping his otherwise useless wings. He repeats his dance again and again, almost mesmerizing the female, squawking loudly all the time. The dance, and the manner in which it is performed, demonstrate good age, good breeding and the overall condition of the father-to-be.

It is important to select the right partner. Dodos are monogamous, which means they mate for life.

Her decision made, the female begins to build the nest with the grass, twigs and leaves provided by the male. The nest is built at ground-level, to a height of about 15 centimetres. The male has even thought to provide his mate with a gizzard stone for her own personal use.

OCTOBER–DECEMBER: THE WET SEASON.

Though cyclones are a danger during this period, the strong winds would bring down (or wash up) a variety of foodstuffs normally unavailable to the dodo. Male dodos start gathering up grass, palm leaves and other materials for nest building.

JANUARY–FEBRUARY: MATING.

Dodo males are visual, noisy and violent. Competition for a mate is fierce, and angry

MARCH–APRIL: CHICKS ARE BORN.

Dodos lay only a single egg each year. Both the male and female will incubate and protect the egg over the seven weeks it will take to hatch. This is the most dangerous time for the dodo parents. Scavenging seabirds will eagerly swoop on unguarded eggs.

The chick is born naked, but already quite well developed. The female regurgitates a milk-like substance, rich in protein, for the chick, which as a result will grow strong within the first month. The chick will stay with its parents for up to a year as it's slowly weaned of its mother's 'milk'. If the chick is reluctant to leave the nest, the parents will actively drive it away.

MAY–SEPTEMBER: WINTER.

By the time the main growing cycle begins again, their weight will be down to around 10 kilograms. The winter is spent feeding and rearing dodo chicks, a further drain on precious resources.

disputes will flare up between rival males. The dodo's hooked beak could cause a lot of damage, and fossil specimens show multiple fractures from fighting. The male stakes out its territory and lays out nest materials to attract a female.

But the female dodo must still approve both the real estate and the landlord!

Did someone or something disturb this limited breeding cycle?

Were the dodo's ground-level nests a huge liability?

THE BITTER END

We cannot say for sure what drove the dodo to extinction. Even the experts can't always agree. But in the case of the dodo, the evidence is compelling.

What we do know is this:

Before the late 1500s, the dodo had been undisturbed for more than 100,000 years. It had evolved to function perfectly within a given set of environmental conditions. Food was plentiful, there were no predators, and the cycle of life was uninterrupted.

Then humans appeared.

For the first time the dodo was hunted, initially for food and then for its exotic appearance and monetary value back home.

It had, in the years following its discovery, become a scientific sensation. In Europe, wealthy citizens were looking to pay well for new exhibits to feature in their private zoos. In 1601 and 1602 expeditions to Mauritius brought back the first live dodos, and demand was soon high for more of these exotic creatures. Many birds died on the way, unable to survive the arduous sea journey, nearly 10,000 kilometres long. But others did make it back, whereupon they became bizarre curiosities.

This fascination with the bird was short-lived, though, and it seems unlikely that the dodo was gathered in sufficient numbers to completely wipe it out.

The trade in ebony may also have impacted on the dodo's environment, but not in a big way. Large areas of Mauritius were covered by dense, impenetrable rainforest and steep mountains, where no human foot ever trod. All the dodos had to do was move deeper into the jungle.

But with the Dutch settlers came other visitors, whose impact would have been far greater.

The excavations at Fort Hendrik also reveal the bones of cattle, deer, goats, chickens and pigs. None of these was native to Mauritius.

These livestock animals were introduced by the Dutch to provide food for the settlers. Over time, they let the animals run wild on the island. Rats, which had arrived as stowaways in the holds of the Dutch ships, also found their way on to the island.

Pigs particularly were released into the wild, mainly so that they could be hunted for sport. It is these pigs that almost certainly had the biggest impact on the dodo's habitat.

Mauritius, it seems, was a pig paradise (as

well as a pigeon paradise). The rooting animals would have had a devastating effect on the ground-dwelling dodo. Pigs would have competed for food, digging up roots and tubers and devouring fruit. But, perhaps more significantly, it would have trampled through and over the dodos' nesting ground, disrupting the birds' mating cycle.

Pigs would have bred much faster than the dodo (with its one egg per parents per year), and the island was soon overrun. In 1709, a visitor to Mauritius describes a hunt in which 1,500 pigs were bagged in a single afternoon.

This was a catastrophe for the dodo. After thousands and thousands of years of living in peace on Mauritius, in just the space of a few short decades its habitat had been destroyed.

But this was not the end for the dodo. Not quite.

GO EAST

In 1662, a German sailor named Volquard Iversen was shipwrecked on Mauritius. During his six-month stay, he reported seeing no dodos at all, anywhere on the island. Until one day when he was exploring a tiny, remote islet to the extreme east of the island. There he accidentally disturbed a large number of the birds.

Iversen had stumbled across the last dodo colony on the island.

Unable to compete with the pigs and other animals that had invaded their world, the remaining dodos migrated east. They found an isolated spit of land, cut off from the main island by the high tide, where there were no pigs.

But these dodos were just surviving, not thriving. Overcrowded, there was no room to expand their territory. Competition would have been even fiercer than usual, and fighting widespread. The dodo's mating patterns had been thrown into disarray, and as old birds died off there were fewer and fewer young birds to replace them.

The dangers of disease from close inbreeding would have also been heightened. Food was in desperately short supply. And on the unprotected spit, the danger from cyclones would have increased.

Within only one or two generations these incredible birds had disappeared completely. Finally: 'dead as a dodo'.

Verdict: killed off by man (even if indirectly) and pigs. The dodo had simply had it too good for too long, and was unable to adapt.

MORTAL REMAINS

The problem with understanding the dodo is the general absence of good fossil remains. The soil of Mauritius is highly acidic, and most dodo bones simply eroded and crumbled to dust.

Even those birds that were stuffed and exhibited in museums around the world were gradually lost. Elias Ashmole, a noted collector of exotica, had a stuffed dodo on display at the Ashmoleon Museum in Oxford. Disastrously, a curator simply threw the exhibit out in 1755. Only the head and a foot were recovered.

With this lack of physical evidence, it's not surprising that many scientists began to doubt the dodo's existence.

Then in 1865, a Mauritian schoolteacher called George Clarke began excavations (initially for fertilizer!) on an estate called Mare aux Songes. He (and subsequently Theodore Sauzier in 1889) recovered a large number of dodo bones from the site.

But still the image of dodo as fat and lumbering persisted, mainly because subsequent reconstructions were still based on the early Dutch paintings of the bird.

Recently, Andrew Kitchener, a curator at the Royal Museum of Scotland, was commissioned to re-create the dodo as faithfully as possible. He tested bone strengths, drew modern comparisons, and used as his model the very first drawings of the dodo. His dodo was much more streamlined and upright.

The possibility of cloning a live dodo has even been raised. Once the key genes have been isolated that made the dodo unique, genetically engineered DNA (the coding that is the basis of all living creatures) could be put into the nucleus of a pigeon's egg.

There's a lot of work and research still to be done, but who knows? One day we may get to meet a live dodo… and then we'll need a new expression for extinct animals!

THE GREAT AUK

Fast Facts

great auk
(*Pinguinus impennis*)

Hydrodynamic

Moved at amazing speeds through the water. Its wings and feathers provided it with minimum drag.

Eyes!

Its specially adapted eyes could focus underwater and see fish at great depths in murky conditions.

Beak!

Very strong and powerful, used for catching, carrying and slicing its prey.

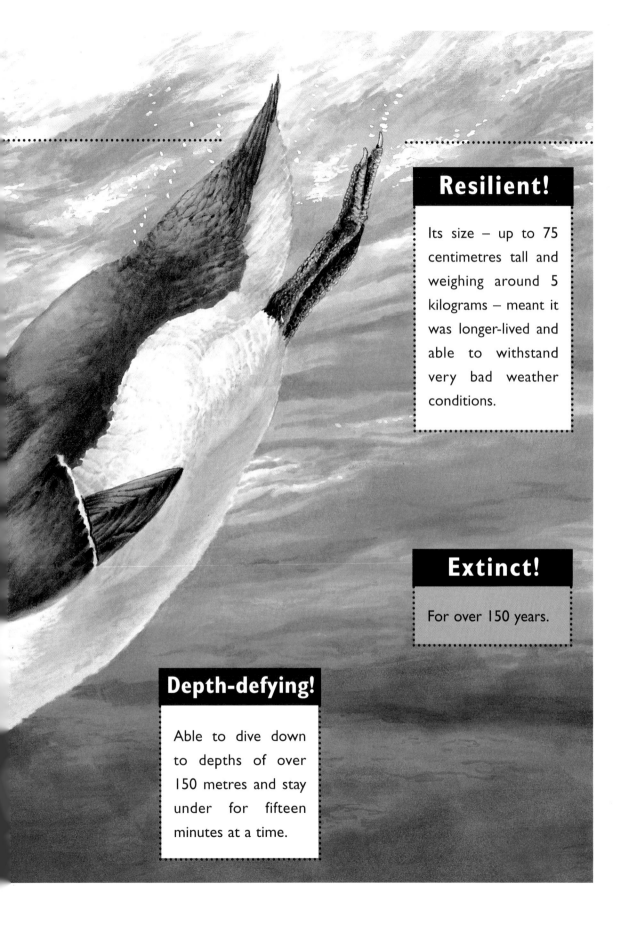

Resilient!

Its size – up to 75 centimetres tall and weighing around 5 kilograms – meant it was longer-lived and able to withstand very bad weather conditions.

Extinct!

For over 150 years.

Depth-defying!

Able to dive down to depths of over 150 metres and stay under for fifteen minutes at a time.

PENGUIN OF THE NORTH

Like the dodo, the great auk has become something of an icon of extinction. Also like the dodo, this remarkable seabird and superbly evolved underwater hunter is largely misunderstood and misrepresented.

The general view of the great auk as, well, not very great at all, is based on its somewhat awkward appearance and clumsy gait on land. In the sea, however, it was a very different matter.

The great auk is a part of the Alcidae family of seabirds. Though it was originally called a penguin, and did resemble modern penguins, it was in fact quite different. For a start, great auks only ever inhabited the northern hemisphere (as opposed to modern penguins, which are exclusive to more southerly areas of the globe). Auks were also bigger and had been around long before today's penguins.

The development of these two similar, but otherwise unconnected, species is an example of co-evolution. Different environment, different ancestry, but an almost identical progression from flying bird to flightless diving seabird.

The Alcidae family includes such seabirds

> Bigger than penguins, auks lived on the opposite side of the world.

as the common puffin and razorbill, but the great auk's nearest relative is actually the guillemot. Still widespread today, the guillemot is about a fifth the size of the great auk and can fly. The earliest known species of this larger, flightless seabird (*Pinguinus alfrednewtoni*) appeared some 5 million years ago, and inhabited an area around North Carolina, USA. The great auk evolved over 500,000 years ago.

What the great auk lost (its ability to fly), it gained in terms of its size. Though clumsy and slow on land, its bulk made it ideally suited to diving for food at sea.

Bigger equals a slower metabolic rate, so the great auk could conserve large amounts of bodily energy and look forward to an extended life (twenty to twenty-five years).

Other evolutionary refinements included short, muscular wings, perfect for reducing friction and slicing through the water. A thick layer of insulating fat meant it could survive icy waters and driving, north Atlantic winds. It even had individual feather muscles, so that the feathers themselves could be pressed

The auk's closest relative is the guillemot, which still exists today.

the northern hemisphere. But while it spent most of its life at sea, it still needed to come ashore to breed.

tight to the body. This way, the great auk could trap less air, and reduce unwanted buoyancy. The great auk was one of the greatest diving birds in the history of the world – it could dive deeper and for longer than any bird in

Is this where it went wrong?

Was the great auk's dominance at sea outweighed by its vulnerability on land?

FUNK FOOD

Some 65 kilometres off the coast of Newfoundland lies a barren, inhospitable chunk of rock nearly a kilometre long and about half a kilometre wide. Its stark granite cliffs are lashed with the full force of north Atlantic gales, driving rain, fog and angry seas. Treacherous currents ebb and flow around its jagged shoreline, and the sea itself is icy and forbidding.

But for the great auk, it was home.

Funk Island, as it is known today, was one of the key breeding grounds of the great auk for many thousands of years. Originally discovered in the early 1500s by local fishermen, it was originally dubbed Isla de Pitigoen, or Island of Penguins. It was later renamed Funk Island because of the ever-present and highly unpleasant smell of ammonia, which came from the uric acid in literally tons of bird excrement.

The sight that greeted those first fishermen must have been incredible: over 100,000 pairs of great auks jammed shoulder to shoulder on its flat-topped cliffs.

PICTURE THE SCENE…

It is early June on Funk Island, and every available inch of rock is covered by mated pairs of great auks. The numbers seem countless, a sea of shuffling feathers and endlessly twitching heads. The birds are packed so tight, it seems incredible that those closest to the cliff edges aren't simply knocked off.

From the boats, fishermen watch as the shifting mass of birds ebbs and flows. There is almost constant motion as male and female

birds alternate between incubating their single egg and going in search of food.

High on the flat-topped cliffs of Funk, one great auk is pushing and shoving its way to the cliff edge. It walks upright, with its head elevated. Its clumsy shuffle is partly due to its weight, but also because its legs are set so far back on its body that it seems always on the verge of toppling over. Its wings are tiny compared to its stocky body – and yet they are clearly wings, rather than flippers, as other diving seabirds have developed.

Its plumage is a dark, blackish brown on its upper surfaces, with a white underbelly and white oval patches under each eye. Its short, pointed tail has a cluster of some fourteen jutting feathers. Its most imposing

feature, though, is its enormous beak. Long, curved, with a number of grooves running along it, it's a formidable weapon.

The great auk reaches the cliff edge and, with almost no pause at all, dives smoothly off.

Underwater now, the great auk is in its element. The fishermen see it flash briefly past them at depth. Though there are six of them and they are rowing with all hands, the auk is faster.

The fishermen are long gone when at last the auk surfaces, a huge herring clamped in its vice-like beak. It will let the tide wash it ashore on Funk, riding the surf in. Then it will begin the long climb back up to its nesting spot.

Quite how it managed to dive to such depths and stay submerged for so long is still largely a mystery. As an air-breathing creature, it would have to hold its breath for fifteen minutes or more. It would also have had to overcome the increased underwater pressure and be able to see in almost pitch black conditions.

Scientists believe that the auk was able to slow its metabolism down to such an extent that it needed very little oxygen to survive. What it did take down with it was then routed to the most vital organs. Auks also had eyes that could focus underwater, maximizing any available light. Out of the water, however, its eyesight may have suffered.

But was its short-sightedness on land an example of evolutionary short-sightedness?

RIGHT PLACE, WRONG TIME

Though the great auk spent only one or two months out of twelve on dry land, this time was fraught with danger.

Auks needed a very specific type of breeding ground. The site had to be large enough to accommodate a huge number of birds at a time, and also far enough off the mainland to escape the attentions of predators such as polar bears. This island further needed to have low, flat-topped cliffs and, because the auk couldn't fly, it needed a sloping approach that was accessible from the shore on foot.

Funk Island was perfect in all respects.

But while polar bears may no longer have been able to gain access to the auk's breeding grounds, another predator simply had to row ashore and take its pick. Humans had arrived on Funk.

As early as 1536, the Grand Banks were known to seafarers as far afield as England, Spain and Portugal. The long and often hazardous journeys to the edge of the known world inevitably left a shortage of food aboard ship, and the sailors would arrive hungry and malnourished. Funk Island, because of its position, was the perfect place to stop and supplement ships' rations.

Huge numbers of great auks were taken by those early sailors. Small boats would return from the island laden six deep and full from bow to stern with auks. The sheer number of birds on the island, and their need to stay with their eggs, meant that pickings were always good.

Funk had essentially become one big larder.

And it didn't stop there. Auks were also gathered for their feathers (which were velvety and soft), their fat (for burning as fuel) and even just to be used as fish bait. Eggs were also consumed for essential protein.

But the worst was yet to come. What began as simply supplementing meagre ships' rations was to become an industry.

GROWING PAINS

From early May, islands such as Funk were colonized by thousands upon thousands of great auks. Male and female birds gathered there to mate. Each pair produced only one egg between them. We know little about the courtship and mating rituals of the great auk, but some people who saw the birds wrote about them.

PICTURE THE SCENE...

It's early May on Funk Island, and thousands of great auks are coming ashore to breed. Above, on the cliff top, a male auk approaches a potential female partner.

The courtship ritual begins with both auks shaking and bobbing their heads vigorously, showing the white patches in front of their eyes, the beak markings and the colourful insides of their mouths. A low gurgling sound accompanies this opening display.

The male then begins to tap his beak against the female's, and they begin to preen each other, running their beaks along each other's feathers, ruffling and cleaning as they go. This is an important social ritual, and helps to keep the feathers waterproof. It is also the final prelude to mating and egg laying.

Eggs are incubated for around six weeks, and male and female auks take turns to warm, protect and turn the egg. There's no nest as such, the birds standing upright over them. The eggs themselves are pear-shaped, which prevents them rolling away (and potentially off the edge of the cliff!), and distinctively marked with blotches and scribbles. In crowded colonies breeding on cliffs, parents need to be able to identify their one egg among thousands, and each is subtly different.

After hatching, chicks are hurried into the water, often after only one or two days, still with the down they were born with (instead of feathers). If they grow tired, chicks will ride on their parents' backs.

Great auks were highly sociable birds. They fed as a group, migrated together in large numbers, and always gathered together at the same mating grounds, year in, year out.

Did the great auk's preferred method of mating in large groups in only a few locations ultimately doom it to extinction?

THE BITTER END

As always, there are still mysteries and question-marks regarding the disappearance of the great auk. Only 500 years ago, eye-witness reports put the number of birds just at Funk Island in their hundreds of thousands – and there were certainly other great auk colonies. How could so many have disappeared in just 350 years? And were humans the sole culprit, or did the planet itself lend a cruel hand?

What we do know is this:

The situation on Funk Island got progressively worse for the great auk. They were easy prey, and humans increasingly exploited their vulnerability and the sheer number that were available in one location. For 300 years, between May and July, auks were harvested in great numbers as they came ashore to breed. From simply being a ready source of available food for passing ships, they became a commodity – a product to be harvested on a mass scale.

Huge stone pens were built by fishermen, and the auks were driven into these in their hundreds. Once there, they were kept packed tight until they were scheduled for slaughter. The birds were killed for their meat, boiled for their fat, and stripped of their feathers. Huge fires were built, fuelled – in the absence of any local wood – by the birds' bodies themselves.

In 1785 Captain George Cartwright, who was among the first colonists in nearby Labrador, spoke out against the carnage and mass slaughter. He alone, it seems, saw where this was going. It wasn't simply that the auks were being killed in great numbers – they were being prevented from breeding normally. Future generations were threatened.

Cartwright's plea on behalf of the great auks was finally heard, and soon afterwards a proclamation was issued. The killing of auks on Funk was at last outlawed. By this time, however, the damage had been done. There was certainly further illegal trade in auks and their eggs after this point. Whatever the case, by the early 1800s there were no more auks on Funk Island.

But the story of the great auk does not end there.

SUNK WITHOUT TRACE

Funk was not the only breeding colony for great auks. Off the south-west corner of Iceland there was a chain of volcanic islands known as the Geirfuglasker. One of these, Garefowl Island, was home to another huge colony of great auks, and had been for centuries.

Though just 40 kilometres off the coast, Garefowl Island was protected from humankind by treacherous currents and jagged rocks. Also, unlike Funk, it was not on any key shipping routes.

Then, disastrously, the Geirfuglasker chain was rocked by a series of volcanic eruptions and seismic shocks, which ended with the submerging of Garefowl Island. The auks had lost another home.

Survivors of this natural disaster moved on, to a nearby island that had withstood the 'seaquake'. It was called Eldey, and it was far from ideal.

Where Garefowl Island had been inaccessible, Eldey was not. Soon man arrived again, but this time their aim was to catch, not kill. And they came in the name of science rather than commerce.

As word spread of the great auk's rarity, it started a rush to study and classify the bird. Museums, zoos and rich amateur naturalists clamoured for specimens. However, no one quite knew how rare the great auk had become, and the desire to collect and preserve it actually sealed the bird's fate.

Seeing a profit to be made, local fishermen began harvesting auks all over again, this time in the name of science. In their efforts to catch and transport live specimens, many birds were killed. Others died on the long journeys to Europe.

Finally, in 1844, two fishermen came ashore on Eldey in search of specimens. They had been employed by one Carl Siemsen, a dealer in rare specimens. Their search of the island found only one pair of great auks, and both birds were killed as the two men tried to catch them. These were the last great auks ever to be seen by humans.

Verdict: killed by man in the name of commerce and, ultimately, science. The great auk's vulnerability lay in its limited range of breeding grounds.

MORTAL REMAINS

A stark and chilling reminder of the events on Funk can still be seen there today. On high granite clifftops, grass can now be seen growing, and yet the island has no natural soil. The air on Funk is heavy with salt spray, and normally plants would find it almost impossible to get a foothold.

Closer examination of the soil reveals that it is made up entirely of the remains of countless decomposed auks. There were enough of them to rot down over time into rich, organic soil.

The sheer scale of the slaughter on Funk is staggering. Another grim landmark is the remains of the stone pens that the auks were once herded into. There are even blackened deposits from the vast pyres that once burned on the island.

Fossil remains and numerous stuffed auks have nevertheless helped scientists build up a more complete picture of this remarkable bird. Though anatomically similar to the modern penguin, the bones led scientists instead to the guillemot as the auk's nearest descendant. A number of preserved eggs have also been found.

The last two auks caught and killed on Eldey in 1844 are now displayed at the Royal Museum of Copenhagen.

Nowadays, Funk is home to many species of modern seabird. Guillemots and razor-billed auks nest there. Scientists still carefully monitor the birds on Funk, assessing their health and that of waters in which they fish. Eldey, off the coast of Iceland, is now a bird sanctuary, teeming with protected species. Perhaps after all a lesson has been learned from the tragedy of the great auk.

THE TASMANIAN TIGER

Fast Facts

Tasmanian tiger
(*Thylacinus cynocephalus*)

Extinct!

For around 65 years.

Camouflaged!

Distinctive body stripes allowed it to blend in with its surroundings as it lay in ambush. They also gave it the name 'tiger'.

Deadly!

A hugely effective carnivore and predator, It had no real challengers in its native environment.

Jaws!

Immensely powerful. It could open its mouth wide, to an angle of 120 degrees.

Feared!

Its appearance and way of life earned it a formidable reputation.

Relentless!

Its slow metabolic rate meant that it had the endurance to pursue its prey for hours on end. It never gave up.

DOG EAT DOG

In its time, the Tasmanian tiger has been both slandered and acclaimed, denounced and embraced. It's now practically a national icon in its native Tasmania, adorning everything from beer labels to the coat of arms. But it's only a generation or two since the population of Tasmania feared and hated it. Maybe even drove it to extinction.

Despite its name, the Tasmanian tiger is not a tiger at all. In appearance, at least, it was more like a wolf or a dog. It picked up the 'tiger' tag thanks to distinctive dark stripes that ran down its back. Its scientific name, Thylacinus cynocephalus, literally means 'pouched dog with wolf's head'.

'Pouched' because the Tasmanian tiger, or thylacine, was actually a marsupial, like the modern kangaroo or wombat. Marsupials differ from other mammals in that they give birth to their young at a very early and undeveloped stage. The offspring are then reared in an exterior body pouch. Other mammals – including human beings – are what is called placental. This means that their offspring grow more fully inside the womb before birth, nourished by the placenta.

Both marsupials and placentals can be traced back to a creature quite like today's duck-billed platypus. At some point around 100 million years ago they diverged from this common ancestor. But while there was soon

The tiger's latin name, Thylacinus cynocephalus, means 'pouched dog with wolf's head'.

evolutionary distance between them, they were all too often competing for the same geographical space. Marsupials across North America, Europe and Asia were wiped out by the more aggressive, competitive and pack-orientated placentals.

In fact, marsupials and thylacines in particular have had a pretty tough time of it almost everywhere. Left to their own devices, they evolved freely in both South America and Australia. Both continents were isolated at this point in Earth's pre-history. Progressively, though, these remaining marsupial strongholds have been breached.

First, South America became joined to North America via the Panama land bridge. The South American marsupials were subjected to intense pressure by migrating predators and rapidly died out.

As its name suggests the Tasmanian tiger was only ever found on the Australian island of Tasmania.

Aborigines – early humans – settled in Australia around 40,000 years ago. Cave paintings depict thylacines being widely hunted. Then, 2,000 or so years ago, Asian seafarers introduced the dingo to the Australian mainland. Thylacines were unable to compete against these pack-hunting dogs, and were soon extinct there too.

Only on Tasmania did the thylacines survive and thrive. But even here they were not to be left in peace. In 1803, Europeans settled on Tasmania, bringing with them agriculture and sheep. The last refuge of the Tasmanian tiger had been invaded…

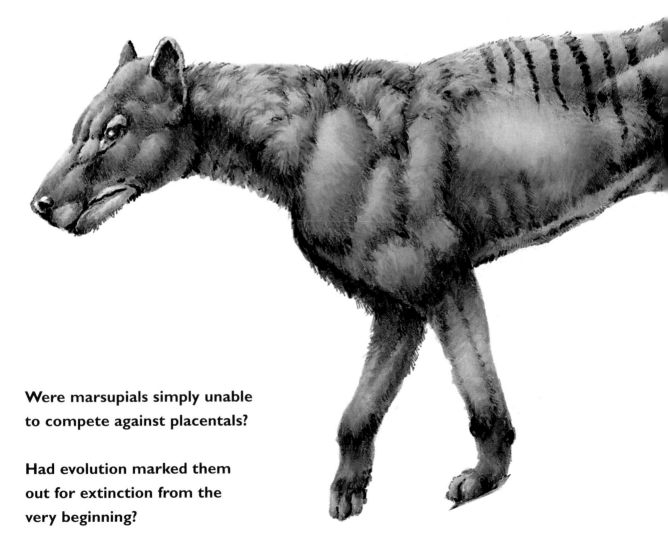

Were marsupials simply unable to compete against placentals?

Had evolution marked them out for extinction from the very beginning?

HUNGRY LIKE THE WOLF

The first European to discover Tasmania, an island state south-east of Australia, was the Dutch explorer Abel Tasman, in 1642. He originally named it Van Diemen's Land, after his sponsor, Anton van Diemen. Size-wise, Tasmania is just slightly smaller than Ireland.

The Tasmanian tiger's favoured hunting grounds were temperate, open areas such as coastal plains and eucalyptus forests. In fact, wherever there was a combination of cover and space, and a plentiful supply of prey...

PICTURE THE SCENE...

The east coast of Tasmania, early evening. The intense heat of the day has passed and in the eucalyptus forest animals are stirring.

From a narrow cave mouth, set in a bowl-shaped depression in the forest floor, a nose appears. Its tip twitches, catching scents of foraging animals well over 30 metres away. More of the sandy-coloured snout appears, followed by a head that is wolf-like and yet at the same time somewhat feline. It tastes the air and yawns, its jaw gaping, revealing all forty or more of its sharp teeth.

The Tasmanian tiger is hungry.

Following well-travelled routes through the undergrowth, it circles round the area it has marked out for tonight's hunt. The gathering dusk is not a problem. Its sharp eyes are well adapted for hunting even in the middle of the night. Its hind legs are long, its front legs shorter, and its feet are slightly oversized. Still, it seems to manage just fine.

Finding exactly the right bit of leafy cover, the Tasmanian tiger settles down to wait. Its striped back helps it blend right in.

Soon there is activity. A wallaby has appeared nearby, foraging for grass and roots around a tall tree. About the size of a big rabbit, and hunched like a kangaroo, the wallaby is unaware of just how close it is to death. The Tasmanian tiger moves forward, but a stray branch impedes its sudden lunge and it drops tantalizingly short of its target. The startled wallaby immediately hops away, darting through the trees as fast as it can go.

Undaunted, the Tasmanian tiger follows. Though it is not as fast as the wallaby, it has endurance and stamina. And once it has the scent, it's like a laser-targeted missile.

The pursuit lasts for hours, well into the night. Exhausted, confused, the wallaby finally stumbles and collapses. Panting, its heart beating furiously, it can only watch as the Tasmanian tiger closes in, its jaws gaping impossibly wide…

The Tasmanian tiger was a fussy eater. Not so much in its choice of prey – there was little it wouldn't hunt and eat. Kangaroos, possums, bandicoots, rabbits, goats, chicken… they were all on the menu. No, it was fussy about what bits of its prey it ate and liked to start with the most tender parts of the kill: the heart, lungs, liver and so on. First it would use its powerful jaws and teeth to crush its prey's throat, killing it. Then it would crack open the animal's rib-cage, taking just the bits it needed and leaving the rest. The Tasmanian tiger never returned to a kill, and didn't scavenge from other carcasses.

The strength of the Tasmanian tiger as a hunter lay in its amazingly low metabolic rate.

It could maintain a long pursuit while burning up relatively little energy. This compensated for its lack of speed. Its huge gape and powerful jaws meant it was superbly equipped as a carnivore.

The Tasmanian tiger was the unchallenged head of the food chain, and there was a plentiful supply of prey. In fact, after 1803, thanks to the European settlers, it could even add sheep to its diet.

And that, ultimately, set it on a collision course with humans.

Did the Tasmanian tiger's ruthless efficiency as a hunter ultimately work against it?

Did human paranoia and distrust breed an atmosphere of fear?

THE LAND OF THE TIGER

After 1803, increasingly large areas of Tasmania were claimed by the European settlers for farmland. Forest areas and the land around them was cleared for grazing and crop growing. Inevitably, all this new farmland intersected with or simply overran the Tasmanian tiger's primary habitat and feeding grounds.

And then there were the sheep. Thousands of them.

From 1830 onwards there was a huge loss of livestock across Tasmania. Thousands of sheep went missing or were killed. But though the Tasmanian tiger certainly accounted for some of these casualties, it wasn't the primary culprit, not by a long way. In fact, the losses were more down to overall bad management, poor choice of land (which was often swampy or exposed) and inadequate fencing. Sheep were poached by native aborigines or escaped convicts, or killed by dogs (actually introduced to Tasmania by the farmers themselves, and then allowed to run wild).

But still the Tasmanian tiger got the blame.

It was a convenient scapegoat. The early reports and sightings, some of which came from escaped convicts (a harsh penal colony was established on the island), fuelled the creature's growing mythical status. A kind of predator hysteria grew on the island, and the Tasmanian tiger was quickly elevated from sheep-eater to man-eater. In truth, there were no records of a Tasmanian tiger ever wilfully attacking a human. They might bite if cornered, but generally they gave humans a wide berth.

Whatever the case, as the hysteria grew, and the claims against the Tasmanian tiger became increasingly inflated, so the cry for action grew. In 1888, the government in Hobart (Tasmania's capital) issued a bounty of £1 per Tasmanian tiger caught or killed.

And suddenly it was open season on Tasmanian tigers.

But did humans actually hunt the entire species to extinction?

...Or did another factor come into play?

GROWING PAINS

The fact is, these often solitary and private animals were rarely observed in the wild. They were trapped, hunted and killed, but hardly ever studied. There are eye-witness accounts (one trapper claimed a wounded thylacine let him tend it, and became friendly towards him), but little is known about its cycle of birth, life and death.

However, scientists have built up a partial picture of this animal by studying its nearest living relative, the Tasmanian devil. Both are marsupials and existed together under similar conditions.

The Tasmanian tiger bred just once a year, probably in December. The female would have courted attention by grovelling and vocalizing through a series of growls and yaps. Though smaller than the male, she was more than capable of seeing off any unwanted attention.

The young were born in January. Being marsupial, they were still undeveloped.

PICTURE THE SCENE...

It's mid-January, and a female Tasmanian tiger carries a full litter of four very young, immature cubs. In her pouch, which faces backwards to avoid damage from grass and plant stems as she walks. They are tiny, hairless, their eyes barely open. It will be another six or seven months until they are strong enough to venture outside.

The female still needs to hunt, despite her burden. She cannot rely on a male to do it for her. The drain on her resources is acute, and if for any reason food is in short supply she may consider jettisoning the cubs. Her survival is paramount – she can breed again this year if necessary.

She settles down to wait under the cover of low, overhanging branches. She needs to make a fast kill, to avoid a lengthy pursuit that will use up her reserves of strength. The next few months will be hard for her, but food is plentiful. All she has to do is wait.

Even after the cubs leave the mother's pouch, they will not be able to fend for themselves for nearly a year. While they are still very small and only just learning to use their legs, the female Tasmanian tiger leaves them hidden in a sheltered place while she hunts. Eventually they will start to follow her, and learn from her. By the next breeding season they will be hunting for themselves.

THE BITTER END

What exactly happened to the Tasmanian tiger is still hotly debated. As usual, the finger is pointed, but in more than one direction. What is true, though, is that a combination of fear and ignorance, and a huge failure to act until it was way too late, brought this once thriving species to the edge of extinction. As to what finally tipped it over, we may never know for sure. But we can certainly point that finger a little more directly.

What we do know is this:

The situation on Tasmania got progressively worse for the Tasmanian tiger through the 1800s and into the 1900s. Sheep ranchers made increasingly preposterous claims about the numbers of sheep lost to tigers. The Van Diemen's Land Company, a big holder of land in the area, claimed to have lost 6,000 sheep in just five years. In 1866, a petition from residents on the east coast claimed that 50,000 sheep per year were being killed by Tasmanian tigers. No attempt to check the validity of these claims was ever made.

Pressure on the government to act increased, and in 1888 the bounty reward system was introduced. For every adult thylacine caught or killed the fee of £1 would be paid (10 shillings, about 50p, for a pup). This was a considerable amount of money in 1888, and the response was huge.

There was already a flourishing trade in Tasmanian tigers, mainly centring on their fur or pelts. But now the trappers and hunters had another reason to increase the volume of animals caught and processed. Farmers too, not exactly gun-shy in the first place, took to actively hunting and killing tigers. In truth, though, few were actually shot. The trappers would lay snares made of hemp along the game trails and capture them alive.

Between 1888 and 1912, around 2,200 thylacines were presented to the government. The trade in thylacine fur increased dramatically. No fewer than 3,500 skins were exported in a twenty-year period. The peak kill for a single year was a total of 172 in 1900. The government was paying out a bounty on a tiger every two days!

Then, in 1906, something changed. The number of thylacines caught dwindled to fifty-eight. By 1909 the total caught was just two. Soon, no tigers at all were being caught. And this dramatic drop in tiger numbers was occurring right across the island, not just where they were being hunted most extensively.

Clearly, something else had struck at the heart of the already stressed Tasmanian tiger population.

SILENT WITNESSES

While the wholesale slaughter of Tasmanian tigers continued, the scientists who perhaps could have stopped it remained strangely silent. Some people in Australia thought that marsupials were inferior to placentals and therefore doomed. They looked at what had happened in other parts of the world, and simply saw the fate of the Tasmanian tiger as a natural progression – essentially unavoidable. Those scientists put almost no political pressure on the government to lift the bounty and protect the species.

In fact, the only thing the scientific community did was to try and get hold of samples of the animal for themselves, paying trappers good money in the process. As it became rarer, so zoos and amateur naturalists got in on the act. All of which did the Tasmanian tiger no good at all. But ultimately, it wasn't the hunters or the collectors that delivered the final blow to the species. It was disease.

By the early 1900s, reports from trappers indicated a strange change in the Tasmanian tiger's behaviour. Captured animals were listless and made little attempt to free themselves. Their overall physical condition was poor. Around this time, other marsupials such as possums and devils were suffering from a devastating, epidemic disease. They showed signs of hair loss, diarrhoea and scabbing. The Tasmanian tiger had developed similar symptoms.

The species was under stress from over-hunting and disease, and yet still the government didn't step in. On 13 May 1930, a Tasmanian tiger was shot and killed on a remote farm. It was the last ever to be seen in the wild.

Verdict: killed by man out of fear and ignorance. Disease may have helped it along, but the damage was already done.

MORTAL REMAINS

Generally, when dealing with extinct animals and piecing together their lives (and deaths), scientists are dealing with bones or mummified remains. Sometimes primitive art survives or, at least in a few more modern cases, photographs. The Tasmanian tiger's disappearance is recent enough for there to be actual film of one.

One of the captured Tasmanian tigers made it to Hobart zoo, where she lived until 1936. Footage taken then still exists today. Her name was Ben, and she's thought to be the last Tasmanian tiger ever. She died of neglect on 10 July 1936. Significantly, the government had only got around to giving the Tasmanian tiger legal protection fifty-nine days earlier.

Way too little, way too late.

Fossilized remains of earlier thylacines have been discovered in Australia, but they are few and far between. One site in West Queensland has yielded six out of the last eight discoveries in the last ten years. Other skulls and teeth have been dated as far back as 25 million years ago. A number of mummified remains have also been unearthed, but these were of more recent animals, around 5,000 years old.

And there are those who don't believe the Tasmanian tiger is extinct at all. To this day, there are reported sightings and supposed evidence of the animals. Several expeditions

have been set up, and huge areas have been thoroughly searched, but still no real trace has been found. Scientists are convinced that if a population had remained after 1930 it would have re-established itself by now. Nevertheless, many believe the Tasmanian tiger is out there somewhere.

Perhaps it's just wishful thinking. Perhaps it's a touch of guilt. Still, they did put it on their national coat of arms.

CONCLUSION

TOO LITTLE, TOO LATE?

SO, WHAT HAVE WE LEARNED?

As a species, not a whole lot. We continue to hunt animals and birds to extinction, pursuing them past the point of no return. But that's only a part of the story, along with the impact humans have on the environment that supports a species.

Our planet is continually changing, and normally these changes occur over vast periods of time, allowing a species to adapt. But if the process is accelerated, then the results can be disastrous. Rapid habitat loss is the primary cause of species endangerment.

Nearly every part of the Earth is affected by humans in one way or another, from the release of greenhouse gases into the environment, the cutting down and burning of huge areas of forest, to the poisoning of fish in polluted waters. The list is endless.

It's easy to sit back and say, 'Well, what can we do?', assuming that these are huge, sweeping changes, out of the hands of the individual. Not true. There's the potential in each and every one of us to make a difference to our environment that will help species including our own survive.

You could...

• *Visit a national park or nature reserve, find out whether there are endangered species and how they are being protected. You may be able to help in local conservation work.*

• *Make sure that if you visit the countryside, you follow the country code. Obey fire regulations, don't drop litter, and leave flowers and birds' eggs where you find them.*

• *Recycle and re-use household items.*

• *Encourage your family to walk or ride a bike to work, or at least take public transport.*

• *Save water by turning off the tap while you brush your teeth, or have a shower instead.*

Plants and animals are the foundation of a healthy eco-system. It's in all our best interests to help preserve species, and allow future generations to experience them too.

In the meantime, sadly, the list of endangered species continues to grow the African elephant, the blue whale, the hybrid spider monkey, the red wolf, the Anatolian leopard, the wild bacterian camel are all under threat at the present time.

Why not see what you can do?